Glory

GLORY

THE DEVOTIONAL

Angelina Herrera

I dedicate this devotional to God, my Abba,
to whom all glory is due.

And to my mother, who showed me that love
has no boundaries. I love you.

A great thanks to Alicia Long, LPC.
Her counseling, coaching, mentoring and helping have
been creative, holistic and empowering.
Thank you, Alicia.

OBOL HOUSE
PUBLISHING COMPANY

An imprint of Huntsville Independent Press

2112 Morningside Drive NW, Huntsville, AL, 35810

Obol House can bring authors to your live event. For more information or to book an event, contact Obol House Publishing Company at +1 (256) 678-0411 or visit our website at: www.ObolHouse.com

Cover design by Chris Treccani - 3 Dog Creative
Interior design by Chris Treccani - 3 Dog Creative

The text for this book was set in Adobe Garamond.

Manufactured in the United States of America
First Obol House paperback edition December 2024

1 2 3 4 5 6 7 8 9 10

The Library of Congress has cataloged the hardcover edition as follows:

Names: NAME, author.

Title: TITLE

LCCN (2024950415)
Identifiers: ISBN 9798992732160 (pbk)

Havens of Worship and Community

https://www.crestbaptistchurch.com/

https://www.thebaseiowa.org/

https://www.salemluth.net/

https://www.facebook.com/TrinityCreston

https://www.facebook.com/
ministerios.mavi.94

https://www.c3andme.com/

Angelina Herrera on YouTube

https://www.youtube.com/
@AngelinaHerrera-so8ho

Hello, I'm Angelina—an Army wife and an Army mom. I'm also a mother to four wonderful children. I truly hope to share with you my love for Psalm 23.

The purpose of this book is to offer a path into scripture—a way to connect with it on a personal level. Just like you might have a favorite song that speaks to your heart, I believe scripture can do the same. It can become something that brings comfort, peace, and meaning. And just as certain words or actions from someone can stay with you for years—changing the way you feel or think—scripture has the power to create those same kinds of lasting memories.

For many years now, I've made it a habit to focus on one verse a day. I'll be honest—there are days when I can hardly remember what happened yesterday. But when I take the time to read the same scripture every day, over weeks or even months, I notice something changes. It stays with me. It becomes part of me.

At the same time, I understand how easy it can be to fall into a routine—to read the same verse every day and feel like you're not getting anything new from it. I've been there. That's why I want to do my best to help you approach it differently.

Think again of your favorite song. You might hum it when you're doing chores, or play it when you need comfort. It becomes a part of your life. I want to encourage you to enjoy scripture in the same way. Let it become familiar and comforting. Let it bring you joy.

Psalm 23 has brought that kind of joy to me—every day. And I want to share that joy with you.

Let's connect together: to God, to His word, to His love, and to His guidance.

I pray that what I've shared helps you feel closer to God—knowing where He is, and understanding what He does in your life.

Enjoy!

Definitions

Affirmation

A spoken or silent expression of agreement, confidence, or support—often used to reinforce belief or truth, either to oneself or to others.
Ex: She gave a quiet smile, a gentle sign that she believed in the words being shared.

Meditation

A focused inward journey of thought or stillness, where the mind turns away from distractions to dwell on deeper understanding, peace, or clarity.
Ex: He sat in silence, letting his thoughts settle like dust in calm air before reaching a decision.

Devotion

A steady commitment marked by care, loyalty, or passionate involvement toward someone or something meaningful.
Ex: Through every challenge, her actions reflected a steadfast devotion that never faded.

Consolation

Providing gentle reassurance or emotional support during moments of sorrow, struggle, or loss—offering presence more than solution.
Ex: His words were few, but the warmth in his voice brought comfort when it was most needed.

Day 1
Psalm 23

1 The Lord is my shepherd: I shall not want. He makes me lie down in green pastures. **2** He leads me beside still waters. He restores my soul. **3** He leads me in paths of righteousness for his name's sake. **4** Even though I walk through the valley of the shadow of death. I will fear no evil. For you are with me. Your rod and your staff, they comfort me. **5** You prepare a table before me in the presence of my enemies; you anoint my head with oil; My cup overflows. **6** Surely goodness and mercy shall follow me all the days of my life, and I shall dwell in the house of the Lord forever. Amen.

Remember: "The Lord is my Shepard"

He is my Father—the one who watches over me with love.

He is my caretaker, tending to my needs with gentleness and strength.

He is my friend, always near, always listening.

He is my advisor, guiding me with wisdom and truth.

Consolation:

Make it a goal to live in the Spirit. Set your heart on joy. You already know the things that lift your spirit—so choose to do them often.

For me, I love cooking. But my family didn't share my enthusiasm for corned beef and cabbage. So, I found a friend who did. That one simple connection brought me joy.

GLORY

Find your own way to stay light-hearted, joyful, and at peace. This is something no one else can do for you. You have to explore your own heart to understand what truly brings you happiness.

At one point, I picked up a book with 300 questions, all asking me: Would this make you happy? The answers surprised me. I discovered joy in places I hadn't expected.

Affirmation:

When you read Psalm 23, you'll see that every single line has the power to speak life into your day. Each verse can be a personal affirmation—something you carry with you, repeat, and believe.

Choose any line that speaks to your heart, and let it echo in your thoughts throughout the day.

Or, if you need a place to start, try this: *I am enough. I have enough.*

Guided Meditations

Speak each meditation aloud for five minutes. Breathe deeply, focus your mind on God's presence, and let each truth settle into your spirit before moving to the next.

Meditation:
"I will give 100% today."

Day 2
Psalm 23

1 The Lord is my shepherd: I shall not want. He makes me lie down in green pastures. **2** He leads me beside still waters. He restores my soul. **3** He leads me in paths of righteousness for his name's sake. **4** Even though I walk through the valley of the shadow of death. I will fear no evil. For you are with me. Your rod and your staff, they comfort me. **5** You prepare a table before me in the presence of my enemies; you anoint my head with oil; My cup overflows. **6** Surely goodness and mercy shall follow me all the days of my life, and I shall dwell in the house of the Lord forever. Amen.

Rest:

Take out a journal and give yourself permission to write whatever is on your heart. Let the words flow—no rules, no pressure. Just be honest with yourself.

When you're done, take a moment to reflect. Then make a list of all the things that bring you hope, peace, joy, and happiness. Big or small, simple or deep—write them down. These are the things that can lift your spirit when you need it most.

Guided Meditations

Speak each meditation aloud for five minutes. Breathe deeply, focus your mind on God's presence, and let each truth settle into your spirit before moving to the next.

GLORY

Meditation:
"My sad days are over."

Day 3
Psalm 23

1 The Lord is my shepherd: I shall not want. He makes me lie down in green pastures. **2** He leads me beside still waters. He restores my soul. **3** He leads me in paths of righteousness for his name's sake. **4** Even though I walk through the valley of the shadow of death. I will fear no evil. For you are with me. Your rod and your staff, they comfort me. **5** You prepare a table before me in the presence of my enemies; you anoint my head with oil; My cup overflows. **6** Surely goodness and mercy shall follow me all the days of my life, and I shall dwell in the house of the Lord forever. Amen.

Remember: "You prepare a table before me in the presence of my enemies."

We've been given freedom—but that freedom comes with structure, not to restrict us, but to keep us safe. Think about a traffic light. The green light is there so we can move forward with confidence and safety.

It's not just about rules or consequences. It's about love, protection, and care.

When we practice doing what's right, we're really practicing grace, kindness, and forgiveness—not just toward others, but also toward ourselves. Even with something as simple as driving, we can choose to respond with patience and compassion.

GLORY

Consolation:

Take a moment to say, "Congratulations."

Thank yourself—for showing up, for holding on, for making it this far. You deserve that recognition.

Give yourself a reward, even a small one. It could have turned out so much differently, but here you are—still standing, still going.

Be proud of yourself. Truly. Let yourself feel that pride and speak it out loud:

"I'm proud of me."

You've come a long way. That matters.

Affirmation:

I have the power to choose. I could take the wrong path—but I choose what is right. I choose to grow, to do better, and to be better.

I am worthy of the good things that come my way.

I deserve the rewards that follow the choices I make in love, truth, and grace.

Guided Meditations

Speak each meditation aloud for five minutes. Breathe deeply, focus your mind on God's presence, and let each truth settle into your spirit before moving to the next.

Meditation:
"I will not be shaken."

Day 4
Psalm 23

1 The Lord is my shepherd: I shall not want. He makes me lie down in green pastures. **2** He leads me beside still waters. He restores my soul. **3** He leads me in paths of righteousness for his name's sake. **4** Even though I walk through the valley of the shadow of death. I will fear no evil. For you are with me. Your rod and your staff, they comfort me. **5** You prepare a table before me in the presence of my enemies; you anoint my head with oil; My cup overflows. **6** Surely goodness and mercy shall follow me all the days of my life, and I shall dwell in the house of the Lord forever. Amen.

Rest:

God cares deeply for you. So if there's anything heavy on your heart—anything that's weighing you down—take a moment right now to talk to Him.

Ask Him to show you the way. Let Him lead you toward the strategy that brings real solutions. Let Him guide you through the pain of a broken relationship. Let Him teach you how to close the doors that no longer lead you closer to Him. Let Him be the one who answers the questions that linger in your soul.

You might be wondering, How?

Start with worship. Not necessarily with lyrics or songs—sometimes, it's just music without words. It's about creating an atmosphere where your heart can drift, reflect, and listen.

GLORY

Think of those moments when you're in the shower, lost in thought. Or on a long drive, just you and the quiet road ahead. That's where God can meet you.

Find what works for you—and let Him in.

Guided Meditations

Speak each meditation aloud for five minutes. Breathe deeply, focus your mind on God's presence, and let each truth settle into your spirit before moving to the next.

Meditation:

"I will not be afraid."

Day 5
Psalm 23

1 The Lord is my shepherd: I shall not want. He makes me lie down in green pastures. **2** He leads me beside still waters. He restores my soul. **3** He leads me in paths of righteousness for his name's sake. **4** Even though I walk through the valley of the shadow of death. I will fear no evil. For you are with me. Your rod and your staff, they comfort me. **5** You prepare a table before me in the presence of my enemies; you anoint my head with oil; My cup overflows. **6** Surely goodness and mercy shall follow me all the days of my life, and I shall dwell in the house of the Lord forever. Amen.

Remember: "He makes me lie down in green pastures."

God delights in me. He enjoys my presence—just as I am.

He creates the perfect place for me to rest, to grow, to love, and to truly live. A place of peace, renewal, and safety—designed just for me.

Consoling: You are so loved. You are such good company. The Lord loves you.

Affirmation:

I am deeply valuable to the One who is the source of all creativity, wisdom, brilliance, and wonder. To Him—I matter. And that means everything.

GLORY

Guided Meditations

Speak each meditation aloud for five minutes. Breathe deeply, focus your mind on God's presence, and let each truth settle into your spirit before moving to the next.

Meditation:

"I will accept what God has for me to strengthen my faith."

Day 6
Psalm 23

1 The Lord is my shepherd: I shall not want. He makes me lie down in green pastures. **2** He leads me beside still waters. He restores my soul. **3** He leads me in paths of righteousness for his name's sake. **4** Even though I walk through the valley of the shadow of death. I will fear no evil. For you are with me. Your rod and your staff, they comfort me. **5** You prepare a table before me in the presence of my enemies; you anoint my head with oil; My cup overflows. **6** Surely goodness and mercy shall follow me all the days of my life, and I shall dwell in the house of the Lord forever. Amen.

Rest:

Take a moment to think about how you can give yourself the most rest today.

Is there something you could organize or rearrange to create more space for peace? Could you take the day off? Is there something you could ask someone to help you with, just to lighten the load?

Ask yourself meaningful questions. Do you need to set aside time to grieve someone you've lost?

I did. My brother passed away at the age of 39. He loved being out on the baseball field—so I began spending time there.

When I gave myself permission to grieve for just one reason, to feel one layer of that loss, I came away lighter. It gave me a sense of clarity and peace I didn't expect.

So ask yourself: What do you need rest from? Take your time. Let God meet you there.

Guided Meditations
Speak each meditation aloud for five minutes. Breathe deeply, focus your mind on God's presence, and let each truth settle into your spirit before moving to the next.

Meditation:
"When I don't understand, I will trust that
God is taking care of it."

Psalm 23

1 The Lord is my shepherd: I shall not want. He makes me lie down in green pastures. **2** He leads me beside still waters. He restores my soul. **3** He leads me in paths of righteousness for his name's sake. **4** Even though I walk through the valley of the shadow of death. I will fear no evil. For you are with me. Your rod and your staff, they comfort me. **5** You prepare a table before me in the presence of my enemies; you anoint my head with oil; My cup overflows. **6** Surely goodness and mercy shall follow me all the days of my life, and I shall dwell in the house of the Lord forever. Amen.

Remember: "He leads me in paths of righteousness for his name's sake."

God is like my divine dispatch—sending guidance when I need direction.

He teaches me not only what is right to do, but also when to do it. His timing and His wisdom work hand in hand.

I'm learning to see things from new perspectives so I can stay committed to what I'm called to do.

Righteousness is part of my responsibility. It means being mindful, showing up, and taking care of the things in my life with purpose and intention.

GLORY

Consolation:

I love myself—and I choose to show that love by taking care of my responsibilities. When I do, it's such a beautiful reminder of what I'm capable of. I begin to see the ways I can show up well for myself—and in doing so, I become better for those around me too.

I've made a promise to care for myself, to protect my peace, and to look out for my well-being.

This realization came from God. One day, He gave me an image: I was like a car, and I was constantly wearing it down—neglecting it, pushing it too hard, beating it up.

Take a moment and listen to your self-talk. Is it gentle? Is it kind? Let God help you see yourself the way He sees you—with love, patience, and care.

Affirmation:

I am trustworthy. I have learned from my past, and I continue to grow with each step I take. I will stay committed to my responsibilities—because growth is not just behind me, it's still ahead of me.

Guided Meditations

Speak each meditation aloud for five minutes. Breathe deeply, focus your mind on God's presence, and let each truth settle into your spirit before moving to the next.

Meditation:

"I will fulfill my responsibilities."

Day 8
Psalm 23

1 The Lord is my shepherd: I shall not want. He makes me lie down in green pastures. **2** He leads me beside still waters. He restores my soul. **3** He leads me in paths of righteousness for his name's sake. **4** Even though I walk through the valley of the shadow of death. I will fear no evil. For you are with me. Your rod and your staff, they comfort me. **5** You prepare a table before me in the presence of my enemies; you anoint my head with oil; My cup overflows. **6** Surely goodness and mercy shall follow me all the days of my life, and I shall dwell in the house of the Lord forever. Amen.

Rest:

Today, give yourself the gift of tending to the things that help you feel whole—especially the things that shift your focus away from appearances and back to your true beauty.

Clear out the distractions. Make space to really see yourself—not just in the mirror, but in the way the Lord created you: wonderfully and intentionally.

If there are things that help you feel more like you—go ahead and do them. Wax your brows, touch up your hair, paint your nails. If buying a piece of shapewear helps you feel more comfortable and confident, then give yourself that grace.

This matters. Taking care of yourself isn't vanity—it's part of honoring the vessel God gave you.

When you feel better within yourself, you'll be freer to focus on the things that truly matter to you. And you'll do them with greater joy, strength, and confidence.

Guided Meditations

Speak each meditation aloud for five minutes. Breathe deeply, focus your mind on God's presence, and let each truth settle into your spirit before moving to the next.

Meditation:
"I have a whole new life."

Day 9
Psalm 23

1 The Lord is my shepherd: I shall not want. He makes me lie down in green pastures. **2** He leads me beside still waters. He restores my soul. **3** He leads me in paths of righteousness for his name's sake. **4** Even though I walk through the valley of the shadow of death. I will fear no evil. For you are with me. Your rod and your staff, they comfort me. **5** You prepare a table before me in the presence of my enemies; you anoint my head with oil; My cup overflows. **6** Surely goodness and mercy shall follow me all the days of my life, and I shall dwell in the house of the Lord forever. Amen.

Remember: "He restores my soul"

Your God—the Creator of oceans and rivers—also created you. Your Father formed you with care and intention, and He's already given you everything you truly need.

So as you go about your day—even something as simple as shopping—take a moment to reflect on what you already have.

Let gratitude rise in your heart. And remember: there is still so much more He has in store for you.

Consolation:

It's easy to focus on what we lack—to dwell on what we don't have. But what's not always easy is pausing to make a list of all the blessings we do have—especially before we go out and buy anything new.

GLORY

Sometimes, we need to give ourselves a different way to think. A new perspective can pull us back to what's real and steady.

It's in that quiet moment of reflection that we find peace—and often, contentment.

Affirmation:

I have all that I will ever need.

Guided Meditations

Speak each meditation aloud for five minutes. Breathe deeply, focus your mind on God's presence, and let each truth settle into your spirit before moving to the next.

Meditation:

"I will embrace a new perspective."

Day 10
Psalm 23

1 The Lord is my shepherd: I shall not want. He makes me lie down in green pastures. **2** He leads me beside still waters. He restores my soul. **3** He leads me in paths of righteousness for his name's sake. **4** Even though I walk through the valley of the shadow of death. I will fear no evil. For you are with me. Your rod and your staff, they comfort me. **5** You prepare a table before me in the presence of my enemies; you anoint my head with oil; My cup overflows. **6** Surely goodness and mercy shall follow me all the days of my life, and I shall dwell in the house of the Lord forever. Amen.

Rest:

Is there someone you've been meaning to call? Someone you've felt nudged to visit? Maybe there's a place you've wanted to volunteer—or a few things you've been putting off mailing.

Rest doesn't look the same for everyone. For each of us, there's something unique that brings joy—and from that joy, we find true rest.

Sometimes rest means reconnecting. Sometimes it means completing a task that's been weighing on your heart. And sometimes, it means making a plan for what's ahead.

Is it time to start saving for that dream career or vacation? This could be your moment to begin building a future that holds more peace and space to breathe.

Whatever rest looks like for you—trust yourself to take that step.

Guided Meditations

Speak each meditation aloud for five minutes. Breathe deeply, focus your mind on God's presence, and let each truth settle into your spirit before moving to the next.

Meditation:

"I have the mind of Christ."

Day 11
Psalm 23

1 The Lord is my shepherd: I shall not want. He makes me lie down in green pastures. **2** He leads me beside still waters. He restores my soul. **3** He leads me in paths of righteousness for his name's sake. **4** Even though I walk through the valley of the shadow of death. I will fear no evil. For you are with me. Your rod and your staff, they comfort me. **5** You prepare a table before me in the presence of my enemies; you anoint my head with oil; My cup overflows. **6** Surely goodness and mercy shall follow me all the days of my life, and I shall dwell in the house of the Lord forever. Amen.

Remember: "Surely goodness and mercy shall follow me all the days of my life"

God is full of compassion and empathy. He sees every need we have, even the ones we don't speak aloud.

Can you remember a time when someone truly thought of you? A moment that made you pause and wonder, Why would they go out of their way for me?

I remember a time when I was working as a housekeeper. One day, a customer canceled on me. I accepted it and went on with my day as usual. At the time, I was also working as a cashier at a grocery store.

To my surprise, that same customer showed up at the store—not to shop, but to find me. She handed me payment, even though I hadn't cleaned her house that day. She looked me in the eye and said, "You still took the time to come by—and I appreciate you."

That moment stayed with me. It reminded me how much thoughtfulness matters. And it reminded me that God often shows His compassion through people—at just the right time.

Consolation:

Your kindness is kept track of. God will find ways to chase you and bless you.

Affirmation:

The kind things I do truly matter. My actions—when done with love and sincerity—leave an impact. I will honor my word. I will keep my commitments, because what I do with kindness carries meaning.

Guided Meditations

Speak each meditation aloud for five minutes. Breathe deeply, focus your mind on God's presence, and let each truth settle into your spirit before moving to the next.

Meditation:
"Don't push—surrender to God."

Day 12
Psalm 23

1 The Lord is my shepherd: I shall not want. He makes me lie down in green pastures. **2** He leads me beside still waters. He restores my soul. **3** He leads me in paths of righteousness for his name's sake. **4** Even though I walk through the valley of the shadow of death. I will fear no evil. For you are with me. Your rod and your staff, they comfort me. **5** You prepare a table before me in the presence of my enemies; you anoint my head with oil; My cup overflows. **6** Surely goodness and mercy shall follow me all the days of my life, and I shall dwell in the house of the Lord forever. Amen.

Rest:

Whatever rest looks like for you, give yourself permission to take it. Whether it's a few quiet moments alone or a full day to pause—embrace the kind of break that truly refreshes your spirit.

As much as possible today, put your needs first. Value yourself enough to say, "I'm busy," and mean it.

Because you are worthy of rest. And today, it's okay to make yourself the priority.

Guided Meditations

Speak each meditation aloud for five minutes. Breathe deeply, focus your mind on God's presence, and let each truth settle into your spirit before moving to the next.

GLORY

Meditation:
"I will make time for God's plan."

Psalm 23

1 The Lord is my shepherd: I shall not want. He makes me lie down in green pastures. **2** He leads me beside still waters. He restores my soul. **3** He leads me in paths of righteousness for his name's sake. **4** Even though I walk through the valley of the shadow of death. I will fear no evil. For you are with me. Your rod and your staff, they comfort me. **5** You prepare a table before me in the presence of my enemies; you anoint my head with oil; My cup overflows. **6** Surely goodness and mercy shall follow me all the days of my life, and I shall dwell in the house of the Lord forever. Amen.

Remember: "Even though I walk through the valley of the shadow of death."

The shadow of death can be many things. It's anything that settles over us like darkness—anything we've come to accept that makes us feel defeated or overwhelmed. For me, that shadow was watching my best friend lose their memory.

I remember how my friend would talk about the fear of forgetting—how hard it was to let go of names, moments, and pieces of themselves that once felt so solid. My heart ached for them.

There are so many things in life that are simply beyond our control. And yet—even in that valley, even under that shadow—God walks with us.

GLORY

Consolation:

Take joy in the small, beautiful moments. Savor them when they come, because the truth is… we don't always get a next time. Let yourself be present. Let yourself enjoy what you can, while you can.

Affirmation:

I have lived joyfully—I've had moments that were truly mine, and no one can take those from me. Even if I am forgotten, I will keep loving. I will keep giving.

Because the value of my heart isn't measured by who remembers me, but by how deeply I choose to live.

Guided Meditations

Speak each meditation aloud for five minutes. Breathe deeply, focus your mind on God's presence, and let each truth settle into your spirit before moving to the next.

Meditation:
"I love myself."

Day 14
Psalm 23

1 The Lord is my shepherd: I shall not want. He makes me lie down in green pastures. **2** He leads me beside still waters. He restores my soul. **3** He leads me in paths of righteousness for his name's sake. **4** Even though I walk through the valley of the shadow of death. I will fear no evil. For you are with me. Your rod and your staff, they comfort me. **5** You prepare a table before me in the presence of my enemies; you anoint my head with oil; My cup overflows. **6** Surely goodness and mercy shall follow me all the days of my life, and I shall dwell in the house of the Lord forever. Amen.

Rest:

This is the moment you've been preparing for—the test you've quietly trained through all your practice and patience. Sometimes, the answers we seek don't come from doing more. They come when we pause—when we rest, breathe, and let peace settle in.

Find a quiet place. Take out a notebook. No music, no distractions—just stillness. Let this be a time where you choose not to be busy. Let your thoughts wander. Let your spirit settle.

Write what comes. Pay attention.

Use this space to get to know yourself better—and to listen for the quiet answers God may be waiting to give you.

GLORY

Guided Meditations

Speak each meditation aloud for five minutes. Breathe deeply, focus your mind on God's presence, and let each truth settle into your spirit before moving to the next.

Meditation:

"I am in God's hands."

Psalm 23

1 The Lord is my shepherd: I shall not want. He makes me lie down in green pastures. **2** He leads me beside still waters. He restores my soul. **3** He leads me in paths of righteousness for his name's sake. **4** Even though I walk through the valley of the shadow of death. I will fear no evil. For you are with me. Your rod and your staff, they comfort me. **5** You prepare a table before me in the presence of my enemies; you anoint my head with oil; My cup overflows. **6** Surely goodness and mercy shall follow me all the days of my life, and I shall dwell in the house of the Lord forever. Amen.

Remember: 'He leads me beside still waters."

God is always watching over you. He is near—closer than you think. And because He is near, it becomes easier to be brave. Still waters remind us that peace is possible, even in the middle of uncertainty. With Him beside you, you don't have to face anything alone.

Consolation:

It's not that you'll never feel fear again. Fear will come—it's part of life. But the goal is to release as many fears as you can. Letting go of them, one by one, creates space for relief. It gives you room to breathe. It brings you rest. When we step out of our own way, and stop letting fear lead, we begin to see things more clearly.

GLORY

We see God more clearly.
We see others more gently.
And we begin to live with courage, not hesitation.

Affirmation:

There have been so many times I've faced my fears—and made it through. And now, here comes another chance. Today, I choose to rise again. I will face this fear—and I will overcome it.

Guided Meditations

Speak each meditation aloud for five minutes. Breathe deeply, focus your mind on God's presence, and let each truth settle into your spirit before moving to the next.

Meditation:

"I am not as tired as I think I am."

Day 16
Psalm 23

1 The Lord is my shepherd: I shall not want. He makes me lie down in green pastures. **2** He leads me beside still waters. He restores my soul. **3** He leads me in paths of righteousness for his name's sake. **4** Even though I walk through the valley of the shadow of death. I will fear no evil. For you are with me. Your rod and your staff, they comfort me. **5** You prepare a table before me in the presence of my enemies; you anoint my head with oil; My cup overflows. **6** Surely goodness and mercy shall follow me all the days of my life, and I shall dwell in the house of the Lord forever. Amen.

Rest:

Take a moment today to give yourself the credit you deserve. You've been showing up—maybe you've been walking through this new devotional for 16 days (that's over two weeks!), or maybe you've been holding steady in something that's been difficult for you. Whatever it is, honor it.

Guard your heart today. Protect the progress you've made. And don't forget to pause and say to yourself: "Well done. I'm proud of you."

Because you should be.

Guided Meditations

Speak each meditation aloud for five minutes. Breathe deeply, focus your mind on God's presence, and let each truth settle into your spirit before moving to the next.

Meditation:
Jeremiah 29:11.

Day 17
Psalm 23

1 The Lord is my shepherd: I shall not want. He makes me lie down in green pastures. **2** He leads me beside still waters. He restores my soul. **3** He leads me in paths of righteousness for his name's sake. **4** Even though I walk through the valley of the shadow of death. I will fear no evil. For you are with me. Your rod and your staff, they comfort me. **5** You prepare a table before me in the presence of my enemies; you anoint my head with oil; My cup overflows. **6** Surely goodness and mercy shall follow me all the days of my life, and I shall dwell in the house of the Lord forever. Amen.

Remember: "He makes to lie down in green Pastures"

Always begin by reminding yourself who God is—your Shepherd, your Protector, your Provider. When you remember who He is, it becomes easier to trust what He does.

Challenge yourself to let go. Release the need to control everything. Let God handle what you're ready to hand over—and with time, give Him even more.

Let Him lead you to rest. To peace. To stillness. He knows how to care for you.

Consolation:

Psalm 23 is all about location. Every line places you somewhere—with purpose, with care. There's a path laid out, a plan unfolding. It shows us that God is not distant. He's present. He's watching over you, guiding your steps, keeping track of where you are, and offering help exactly when you need it.

You're never wandering without direction—He's walking with you, every step of the way.

Affirmation:

I am not alone. Help is never far from me—because my God walks with me. When I need something, He's already there—ready to provide, ready to guide.

Guided Meditations

Speak each meditation aloud for five minutes. Breathe deeply, focus your mind on God's presence, and let each truth settle into your spirit before moving to the next.

Meditation:
Psalm 25.

Day 18
Psalm 23

1 The Lord is my shepherd: I shall not want. He makes me lie down in green pastures. **2** He leads me beside still waters. He restores my soul. **3** He leads me in paths of righteousness for his name's sake. **4** Even though I walk through the valley of the shadow of death. I will fear no evil. For you are with me. Your rod and your staff, they comfort me. **5** You prepare a table before me in the presence of my enemies; you anoint my head with oil; My cup overflows. **6** Surely goodness and mercy shall follow me all the days of my life, and I shall dwell in the house of the Lord forever. Amen.

Rest:

Today can be your Pet Day. Take time to relax with your pets—let their presence bring you peace. Set up a pet play date with friends, or surprise someone by sharing treats they can give to their own furry companions. Even keeping a few extra treats in your car to share can be a simple act of kindness.

Rest doesn't always mean doing nothing. Sometimes, it means lifting a little weight off someone else's shoulders—or simply bringing a smile. Showing care is a beautiful way to rest—and it blesses both the giver and the receiver.

Guided Meditations

Speak each meditation aloud for five minutes. Breathe deeply, focus your mind on God's presence, and let each truth settle into your spirit before moving to the next.

Meditation:

Ephesians 6.

Day 19
Psalm 23

1 The Lord is my shepherd: I shall not want. He makes me lie down in green pastures. **2** He leads me beside still waters. He restores my soul. **3** He leads me in paths of righteousness for his name's sake. **4** Even though I walk through the valley of the shadow of death. I will fear no evil. For you are with me. Your rod and your staff, they comfort me. **5** You prepare a table before me in the presence of my enemies; you anoint my head with oil; My cup overflows. **6** Surely goodness and mercy shall follow me all the days of my life, and I shall dwell in the house of the Lord forever. Amen.

Remember: "You prepare a table before me in the presence of my enemies"

Justice isn't something you have to create on your own—it's something the Lord prepares for you. Let Him be the one to set things right. Don't hold on to un-forgiveness. Don't seek revenge or try to match hurt with hurt.

No one carries out justice with more wisdom, mercy, and power than God. Trust His timing. Give Him space to unfold His plan. He sees everything—and He hasn't forgotten you.

Consolation:

I do not believe anyone deserves to be treated unfairly or with disrespect. You are deeply valued. Your thoughts matter. Your voice matters. Your opinions hold weight and worth.

Never forget that your presence is important—and you deserve to be seen and heard with kindness.

Affirmation:

The Lord will take care of it. And I choose to step back and let Him. His hands are steady. His timing is perfect. I trust Him with what I can't control.

Guided Meditations

Speak each meditation aloud for five minutes. Breathe deeply, focus your mind on God's presence, and let each truth settle into your spirit before moving to the next.

Meditation:

"I am love."

Day 20
Psalm 23

1 The Lord is my shepherd: I shall not want. He makes me lie down in green pastures. **2** He leads me beside still waters. He restores my soul. **3** He leads me in paths of righteousness for his name's sake. **4** Even though I walk through the valley of the shadow of death. I will fear no evil. For you are with me. Your rod and your staff, they comfort me. **5** You prepare a table before me in the presence of my enemies; you anoint my head with oil; My cup overflows. **6** Surely goodness and mercy shall follow me all the days of my life, and I shall dwell in the house of the Lord forever. Amen.

Rest:

Make space to dream. Rest isn't only about slowing down—it can also be about planning quiet, meaningful moments for now and for later.

Sometimes, just the act of dreaming or imagining a restful future can bring calm into your present. Let yourself go there. It's worth it. Your peace matters.

Guided Meditations

Speak each meditation aloud for five minutes. Breathe deeply, focus your mind on God's presence, and let each truth settle into your spirit before moving to the next.

GLORY

Meditation:
"I am not missing out."

1 The Lord is my shepherd: I shall not want. He makes me lie down in green pastures. **2** He leads me beside still waters. He restores my soul. **3** He leads me in paths of righteousness for his name's sake. **4** Even though I walk through the valley of the shadow of death. I will fear no evil. For you are with me. Your rod and your staff, they comfort me. **5** You prepare a table before me in the presence of my enemies; you anoint my head with oil; My cup overflows. **6** Surely goodness and mercy shall follow me all the days of my life, and I shall dwell in the house of the Lord forever. Amen.

Remember: "You anoint my head with oil"

You are holy. God has anointed you—chosen you—set you apart for something meaningful and sacred. You are not ordinary. You are treasured. You are precious in His sight. Walk in that truth today. You carry His purpose and His blessing.

Consolation:

You are incredibly valuable. Think of how people keep fine china tucked away in cabinets—those special dishes reserved for meaningful occasions, handled with care and purpose.

I don't mind using dishes as an example—because even in the Bible, God uses simple things to show us how much we matter. He tells us to look at the birds, and how they're cared for. To look at the flowers, clothed in beauty greater than a king's robe.

If God does all that for them—how much more will He do for you?

Affirmation:

I am more valuable than I ever realized. My worth isn't based on what I've done or what others see. It's rooted in who I am, and who God created me to be. I carry more beauty, strength, and purpose than I ever knew.

Guided Meditations

Speak each meditation aloud for five minutes. Breathe deeply, focus your mind on God's presence, and let each truth settle into your spirit before moving to the next.

Meditation:

"I respect God."

Day 22
Psalm 23

1 The Lord is my shepherd: I shall not want. He makes me lie down in green pastures. **2** He leads me beside still waters. He restores my soul. **3** He leads me in paths of righteousness for his name's sake. **4** Even though I walk through the valley of the shadow of death. I will fear no evil. For you are with me. Your rod and your staff, they comfort me. **5** You prepare a table before me in the presence of my enemies; you anoint my head with oil; My cup overflows. **6** Surely goodness and mercy shall follow me all the days of my life, and I shall dwell in the house of the Lord forever. Amen.

Rest:

What can you finish today that will give you more space to enjoy the time ahead? Is it finally checking out those online shopping carts? Wrapping up your grocery list? Maybe it's sitting down to create a budget before payday arrives.

Whatever it is, take a moment to do it now. Sometimes rest means making room for peace later by taking care of the little things today.

Guided Meditations

Speak each meditation aloud for five minutes. Breathe deeply, focus your mind on God's presence, and let each truth settle into your spirit before moving to the next.

GLORY

Meditation:
"I will name all who love me in my life right now."

Day 23
Psalm 23

1 The Lord is my shepherd: I shall not want. He makes me lie down in green pastures. **2** He leads me beside still waters. He restores my soul. **3** He leads me in paths of righteousness for his name's sake. **4** Even though I walk through the valley of the shadow of death. I will fear no evil. For you are with me. Your rod and your staff, they comfort me. **5** You prepare a table before me in the presence of my enemies; you anoint my head with oil; My cup overflows. **6** Surely goodness and mercy shall follow me all the days of my life, and I shall dwell in the house of the Lord forever. Amen.

Remember: "...and I shall dwell in the house of the Lord forever."

If we spend so much time preparing for a place we'll live in for 20 years, how much more should we consider the place we'll live in for eternity? Heaven isn't just a far-off promise—it's our forever home. So let's begin to live with that in mind.

Let's learn the culture of eternity—the language of grace, the attitude of love, the mindset of peace. We've already been accepted into God's house. Now it's time to embrace the overflow of His abundance.

We won't always be living the way we are now—so let's start preparing our hearts to live like we belong where we're going.

GLORY

Consolation:

It's hard to imagine a place where there's no sun—because God Himself is the light. But that's the reality of the eternal home we're promised. A place where His presence shines brighter than anything we've ever known.

It may feel distant or hard to grasp, but it's real, and it's something I want to start preparing my heart for—because that's where I'm going.

Affirmation:

It won't be like this forever. This season is temporary—but my forever home is being prepared. And so, I will prepare too. I'm getting ready for what's eternal.

Guided Meditations

Speak each meditation aloud for five minutes. Breathe deeply, focus your mind on God's presence, and let each truth settle into your spirit before moving to the next.

Meditation:
"I will pray about everything."

Day 24
Psalm 23

1 The Lord is my shepherd: I shall not want. He makes me lie down in green pastures. **2** He leads me beside still waters. He restores my soul. **3** He leads me in paths of righteousness for his name's sake. **4** Even though I walk through the valley of the shadow of death. I will fear no evil. For you are with me. Your rod and your staff, they comfort me. **5** You prepare a table before me in the presence of my enemies; you anoint my head with oil; My cup overflows. **6** Surely goodness and mercy shall follow me all the days of my life, and I shall dwell in the house of the Lord forever. Amen.

Rest:

Take time today to count your blessings. Write down everything that went right—even the small things. List the times you overcame, the moments you won, the savings you found, and the ways provision showed up just when you needed it.

Think about how you met the people you love so deeply. Each connection, each moment, was a gift. Creating an attitude of gratitude is a habit—just like rest. And when you make space for both, your soul will feel lighter, stronger, and more at peace.

Guided Meditations

Speak each meditation aloud for five minutes. Breathe deeply, focus your mind on God's presence, and let each truth settle into your spirit before moving to the next.

GLORY

Meditation:
"No matter what, I will keep moving forward."

Day 25
Psalm 23

1 The Lord is my shepherd: I shall not want. He makes me lie down in green pastures. **2** He leads me beside still waters. He restores my soul. **3** He leads me in paths of righteousness for his name's sake. **4** Even though I walk through the valley of the shadow of death. I will fear no evil. For you are with me. Your rod and your staff, they comfort me. **5** You prepare a table before me in the presence of my enemies; you anoint my head with oil; My cup overflows. **6** Surely goodness and mercy shall follow me all the days of my life, and I shall dwell in the house of the Lord forever. Amen.

Remember: "Surely goodness and mercy shall follow me All the days of my life..."

This promise reminds me to pause and look more closely at how I live. I don't want to overlook or take for granted the mercy that has carried me—again and again.

God's goodness has followed me, even when I didn't notice. His mercy has covered me, even when I didn't deserve it. And now, I want to live with deeper awareness and gratitude for every single day He gives.

Consolation:

Growth begins with paying attention.

Am I kind to the driver in front of me when they slow me down?

GLORY

Have I truly loved my neighbor—not just in words, but in action?

Do I care for my family before I give elsewhere, even to my church?

The answers often reveal themselves in times of stress. Not when everything is easy, but when I'm stretched thin. That's when the truth about how I treat others comes to light. And that's where real growth begins.

Affirmation:

I am willing to change everything I need to. Whatever it takes for me to grow, to heal, to become who I'm meant to be... I will take that step. With God's help, I am ready to become more whole.

Guided Meditations

Speak each meditation aloud for five minutes. Breathe deeply, focus your mind on God's presence, and let each truth settle into your spirit before moving to the next.

Meditation:

"I am debt-free."

Day 26
Psalm 23

1 The Lord is my shepherd: I shall not want. He makes me lie down in green pastures. **2** He leads me beside still waters. He restores my soul. **3** He leads me in paths of righteousness for his name's sake. **4** Even though I walk through the valley of the shadow of death. I will fear no evil. For you are with me. Your rod and your staff, they comfort me. **5** You prepare a table before me in the presence of my enemies; you anoint my head with oil; My cup overflows. **6** Surely goodness and mercy shall follow me all the days of my life, and I shall dwell in the house of the Lord forever. Amen.

Rest:

Give yourself permission to relax today. Do the absolute minimum—let this be a day of true stillness. If guilt starts to creep in, pause and ask God: Is this Your gentle nudge—or am I simply struggling to love myself the way You do?

Either way, let God guide your rest. He knows exactly what your heart needs.

Guided Meditations

Speak each meditation aloud for five minutes. Breathe deeply, focus your mind on God's presence, and let each truth settle into your spirit before moving to the next.

GLORY

Meditation:
"My eternal problems are over."

Day 27
Psalm 23

1 The Lord is my shepherd: I shall not want. He makes me lie down in green pastures. **2** He leads me beside still waters. He restores my soul. **3** He leads me in paths of righteousness for his name's sake. **4** Even though I walk through the valley of the shadow of death. I will fear no evil. For you are with me. Your rod and your staff, they comfort me. **5** You prepare a table before me in the presence of my enemies; you anoint my head with oil; My cup overflows. **6** Surely goodness and mercy shall follow me all the days of my life, and I shall dwell in the house of the Lord forever. Amen.

Remember: "He makes me lie down in green pastures"

When you let God lead, He will lead—and your walk with Him can be full of peace and rest. But if you need to understand every turn, every reason, every outcome… the journey will feel harder. You'll find yourself resisting, struggling to relax into His pace.

Consolation:

Imagine I asked you for a couple of hours of your time, and you said yes. Then we got in the car and went for a drive. You didn't ask where we were going. You simply trusted me. You sat back, stayed patient, and enjoyed the ride.

That's the kind of rest God wants to give you.

GLORY

If you're still finding it hard to let go and trust, I encourage you to watch The Shack. It paints a beautiful picture of how God walks with us, even through the hardest places.

Affirmation:

I can be led. My heart is open, my spirit is willing, and I trust the One who goes before me. I don't have to have all the answers—because I am learning to follow with faith.

Guided Meditations

Speak each meditation aloud for five minutes. Breathe deeply, focus your mind on God's presence, and let each truth settle into your spirit before moving to the next.

Meditation:

"I will take communion."

Psalm 23

1 The Lord is my shepherd: I shall not want. He makes me lie down in green pastures. **2** He leads me beside still waters. He restores my soul. **3** He leads me in paths of righteousness for his name's sake. **4** Even though I walk through the valley of the shadow of death. I will fear no evil. For you are with me. Your rod and your staff, they comfort me. **5** You prepare a table before me in the presence of my enemies; you anoint my head with oil; My cup overflows. **6** Surely goodness and mercy shall follow me all the days of my life, and I shall dwell in the house of the Lord forever. Amen.

Rest:

Take time to deep clean your bedroom today. Make it feel like a sanctuary—a space that welcomes rest, calm, and comfort. Clear the clutter, refresh the space, and let it reflect the peace you're inviting into your life. Your room should feel like yours—a place where you can fully relax and breathe.

Guided Meditations

Speak each meditation aloud for five minutes. Breathe deeply, focus your mind on God's presence, and let each truth settle into your spirit before moving to the next.

Meditation:
"I will study God's Word."

Day 29
Psalm 23

1 The Lord is my shepherd: I shall not want. He makes me lie down in green pastures. **2** He leads me beside still waters. He restores my soul. **3** He leads me in paths of righteousness for his name's sake. **4** Even though I walk through the valley of the shadow of death. I will fear no evil. For you are with me. Your rod and your staff, they comfort me. **5** You prepare a table before me in the presence of my enemies; you anoint my head with oil; My cup overflows. **6** Surely goodness and mercy shall follow me all the days of my life, and I shall dwell in the house of the Lord forever. Amen.

Remember: "Even though I walk..."

Keep walking. Don't stop just because it gets hard. Pausing in the pain only makes it linger. Push through. Rip the bandage off if you must. God isn't offering you a temporary fix—He's inviting you into lasting healing. Trust the process. Healing comes as you move forward, step by step, with Him.

Consolation:

The hard parts of life are never easy—but they're not all bad. Think of a baby cutting their first tooth. It hurts, yes—but that pain is part of something necessary. Something good.

In the same way, when you're going through something tough, try to hold on to a bit of grit, a bit of bite—and a holy kind of

Rest isn't just about sleep. It's about what brings you joy, what makes you feel whole, what gives you a sense of progress or peace. Sometimes, it's catching up on sleep. Sometimes, it's working a second job while listening to your favorite show—because paying your bills brings you peace of mind.

Whatever it looks like for you—enjoy it. Let it restore you. That kind of rest is powerful and guilt-free.

Guided Meditations

Speak each meditation aloud for five minutes. Breathe deeply, focus your mind on God's presence, and let each truth settle into your spirit before moving to the next.

Meditation:
"I believe in God's Word."

Day 31
Psalm 23

1 The Lord is my shepherd: I shall not want. He makes me lie down in green pastures. **2** He leads me beside still waters. He restores my soul. **3** He leads me in paths of righteousness for his name's sake. **4** Even though I walk through the valley of the shadow of death. I will fear no evil. For you are with me. Your rod and your staff, they comfort me. **5** You prepare a table before me in the presence of my enemies; you anoint my head with oil; My cup overflows. **6** Surely goodness and mercy shall follow me all the days of my life, and I shall dwell in the house of the Lord forever. Amen.

Remember: "I shall not want."

I truly have more than I could ever need. God has provided for me in ways seen and unseen. My heart is full. My needs are met. And in His care, I lack nothing that truly matters.

Consolation:

Take a moment to count your blessings. Not just the big ones, but the small ones too. The breath in your lungs. The people who love you. The strength that carried you through what you once thought you couldn't survive.

Gratitude brings comfort. It shifts your heart. And sometimes, it's the very thing that carries you through.

Angelina Herrera

Affirmation:

I am content. Right here, in this moment, I have enough. I am enough. Peace lives in my heart, not in what I'm chasing, and today, that peace is mine.

Maybe you've felt a stirring in your heart—a longing for peace, for hope, or for something deeper that the world just hasn't been able to satisfy. Perhaps you've been searching for love that doesn't fail, for guidance that never fades, or for a sense of purpose that reaches beyond the temporary.

That longing is not an accident. It's God calling to you. He has always seen you, always known you, and always loved you. He's never been far from you, even if you've felt distant.

Right now, you have the opportunity to begin a relationship with Him—not through perfection, not by earning it, but simply by opening your heart and saying yes. It starts with a prayer. If you're ready, here's a simple prayer you can say to invite Jesus into your life, to accept His love, His forgiveness, and His leadership over your life.

If you do not have a relationship with God and you would like to, here is a prayer for you.

Prayer of Salvation
Lord, I recognize that I have sinned.
I believe that Jesus died for my sins and took
my place on the cross.
I believe He rose again on the third day.

Today, I accept Jesus as my Lord and Savior.
Lord Jesus, please come into my heart, my mind, my emotions, and every part of my life. Take over.

GLORY

I submit myself fully to You. I give You my heart, my will, my thoughts, my feelings, and my life. Do with me as You see fit.

Thank You for all You've done and continue to do for me. Teach me to follow You closely, and never let me drift far from You.

In Jesus' Name I pray,
Amen.

If you said this prayer from your heart, then welcome to the family of God. You are now a child of God, deeply loved, fully accepted, and forever His. I celebrate this powerful moment with you, and I want you to know—you are not alone. All of heaven rejoices over you right now, and so do I.

www.ingramcontent.com/pod-product-compliance
Lightning Source LLC
Chambersburg PA
CBHW051644120626
46551CB00015B/2212